ZEN

AMEN

AMEN

ZEN

A COLLECTION OF ABECEDARIANS

BY

MICHAEL KRIESEL

PEBBLEBROOK
PRESS

Published by Pebblebrook Press,
an imprint of *Stoneboat*
PO Box 1254
Sheboygan, WI 53082-1254
Editors: Rob Pockat, Signe Jorgenson, Jim Giese, Lisa Vihos
www.stoneboatwi.com

Zen Amen ©2019 Michael Kriesel
LC Control Number: 2018912212
ISBN: 978-0-578-40151-5

Printed in the US

Acknowledgements

With gratitude to Linda Aschbrenner of *Free Verse* magazine; Karl Elder and his journal *Seems* at Lakeland University in Sheboygan, Wisconsin, both for his example and for his mentorship; Vince Gotera and *North American Review*; *The Entendres* critique group (most notably F. J. Bergmann, Marilyn Taylor, and Wendy Vardaman); the editors of the journals in which many of the poems in this collection appeared; Ben Pierce, for his mentorship in the occult during the mid to late '90s, which led to these poems; Rob Pockat, Signe Jorgenson, Jim Giese, and Lisa Vihos of Pebblebrook Press for catching missing syllables and making this book the best it could be; The Wisconsin Fellowship of Poets; my mom, Virginia Valent; and Mark Zimmermann, whose nudging encouragement led to the dusting-off and publication of this collection.

Honors and Awards:

"Mineral Kingdom" received an honorable mention in *North American Review*'s 2010 Hearst Competition.

"Over the Rainbow" was a finalist in *North American Review*'s 2009 Hearst Competition.

"Abbey Road" was a finalist in *Another Chicago Magazine*'s 2008 competition.

"Secret Women" received an honorable mention in *North American Review*'s 2008 Hearst Competition.

"Zen Amen" was a finalist in *North American Review*'s 2007 Hearst Competition.

Previously published poems:

2010 Rhysling Anthology: "Fungi from Yuggoth"

Arbor Vitae: "Key Lime Christ"

Barbaric Yawp: "Akashic Records," "Amber," "Fungi from Yuggoth," "Sidereal Pendulum," "Zone of Light"

Bramble: "Wisconsin Pyramid"

Chiron Review: "Electronic Voice Phenomenon"

Free Verse: "A Modern Grimoire," "Apprentice," "Astral Projection," "Book of Wonders," "Cell," "Hollow Earth," "Loop in a Field," "Middle Pillar," "New Age," "Office Dervish," "Prince of Trees," "Tarot," "Teen Shaman," "What's Missing," "Where Light Goes," "Xenogenesis," "Zen Amen"

Mobius: The Journal of Social Change: "Black Pyramid," "Viral Savior"

North American Review: "Mineral Kingdom," "Over the Rainbow," "Secret Women," "Zen Amen"

Poemeleon: "Over the Rainbow"

Seems: "Lost & Found," "Serpent Mound," "Sunlight Monster"

*Star*Line*: "Gilgamesh Tomb Found in Iraq"

Stoneboat: "Bestiary," "Levitation Breathing," "The Possessed"

Verse Wisconsin: "Navy Witch"

The Writer: "Abbey Road"

TABLE OF CONTENTS

II.   Doubles

FOREWORD

As arduous forms serve some poets like prescription lenses for astigmatism, one cannot picture with less than omniscient certitude that, in the making of this volume, Mr. Kriesel magnificently magnified his already formidable consciousness through strict adherence to what reigns as the fiercest of formal constraints.

Many, surely, are the seasoned contemporary poets—whether they be ascetics or neo-romantics—who would ascribe incalculable value to such an enervating undertaking as this work, fraught as it is with unnerving though liberating impediments encountered in the act of composition, the means of escape analogous to what Robert Pirsig identifies in *Zen and the Art of Motorcycle Maintenance* as the appropriate response to "stuckness." From the point of view of the poet, that condition is the moment the mind is stood still, forced to stare upon or, on the other hand, to turn away from its metaphysical mountain until the cloud, then the fog, entirely passes and again the mountain beckons. Problem, patience, solution. Conveyed abstractly, in the grandest sense, one might call the method means to transcendence.

What is especially laudable about Mr. Kriesel's climb, if we dare label the artist's aspirations with a moniker so crass, is that he has long ago traversed the foothills and risen above the tree line, scrutinizing now and at successive moments the apogee, which is forever the sheer face of the cliff. The ensuing trudge is deliberate, slow-going, willful, even for observers, whose reward, beside retrospective delight at the turns of lines, may not only be a vicarious rush but memory of mesmerizing spells cast by John Milton and/or James Merrill, more so than by my abecedariums.

A degree in psychology is hardly required to fathom that persons of extraordinary accomplishment often bear an affliction similar to OCD—a thing beyond inspiration, beyond passion, beyond even possession. Perhaps a neologism is necessary to characterize such that is found here, serial ingeniousness in the execution of technique that reads like acts divine at the many rests—our eyes' descent upon the page switchbacks, tracking, paradoxically, the poet's ascent. Perhaps the conceit is overwrought, gaudy artifice on my part. Less honest, however, would be for a reader to deny the preeminent beauty of *Zen Amen*, its footholds transmogrifying to portals, revealing the maze of endless though inevitable associations that make for the mystery of the mind.

Karl Elder
Author of *Mead: Twenty-six Abecedariums*
Lakeland University Fessler Professor of Creative Writing
  & Poet in Residence
February 2018

NOTES ON COMPOSING THESE POEMS

This is a book I wrote ten years ago about something I did twenty years ago. When I was in my mid-forties (2006 – 2008), I was obsessed for an eighteen-month period with the composition of seventy-three abecedarians and double abecedarians, all in a metaphysical vein. With fantastic beginner's luck, my second one, "Zen Amen," ended up a finalist in *North American Review*'s 2007 Hearst Poetry Competition.

I first learned of the form from Karl Elder at Lakeland University in Sheboygan, Wisconsin. We shared a publisher, Linda Aschbrenner's Marsh River Editions. Karl's *Mead: Twenty-six Abecedariums* (Marsh River Editions, 2005) got me started down a pleasantly obsessive road, resulting in some poems I never would have written otherwise. I couldn't have hoped for a better example, as Karl was the first poet to write decasyllabic abecedarians, coining the term "abecedarium" to distinguish his variation on the form.[1]

During the first half of my alphabet binge, I wrote regular or "single" abecedarians that have ten syllables per line, with the exception of "A Modern Grimoire." The only constraint was starting the first line with "A," the second with "B," etc. Or, in the case of a reverse abecedarian, starting the first line with "Z."

At some point during this period, Wisconsin poet Anjie Kokan sent me a few of her own examples in a new form just starting to appear on the internet: the double abecedarian, where each line's final letter (or sound) must also follow the pattern.

So, after composing thirty-four singles in nine months, I upped the ante and went on to write thirty-nine doubles during a second nine-month period, each of which also had ten syllables per line. To the best of my knowledge, I was the first poet to do this. I published a decasyllabic double abecedarian, "Secret Women," in the March/April 2008 issue of *North American Review*, and no examples of this more challenging variation appeared in the 2000 – 2009 editions of either *The Best American Poetry* anthology or *The Pushcart Prize Best of the Small Presses* series. My internet searches have also failed to yield examples of decasyllabic double abecedarians other than my own; the only other double abecedarians I've found have varying numbers of syllables per line.

From necessity, I quickly gave myself leeway for fudging as I wrote the doubles. For instance, I softened the rules to let "cue" or "queue" stand in for "Q." Or "blue jay" for a line ending in the letter "J."

The problem with doubles comes in when you realize that we memorize words by their first letter, not their last. When was the last time you thought of four words ending with "J"? After writing a few of these, I saw a need for a "reverse dictionary." No such thing existed in 2007 (and maybe still doesn't), so I had to make one.

I found a website where I could type in a number of blanks with a designated letter, such as "???Z," and it would spit out a list of all possible combinations of four letters with "Z" as the last. Not all of these were words, of course, so later on I'd highlight the actual words. For half an hour every night at work, on break from my janitor job at a small rural elementary school, I'd enter word parameters and print the pages. After a few weeks, I had a three-ring binder of word lists. I wrote thirty-nine double abecedarians during a nine-month period. Admittedly, some were disjointed or fragmentary, though four were finalists or honorable mentions in the 2007 – 2010 Hearst contests.

Working this form encouraged me (again, from necessity) to trust taking greater conceptual leaps in my poems. You really have to jump from rock to rock in these, packing a lot in each line, with all the different bases you need to hit in short spaces. They often move at breakneck pace, with larger-than-normal gaps between ideas and images.

At the time I was writing these poems, I was pretty much a writing monk, living alone in a small house in rural central Wisconsin and working four hours each evening as a janitor, a job intentionally chosen for its low mental stress. Four hours each morning went into writing and revising these poems as well as reviewing poetry books for Len Fulton's *Small Press Review*, taking part in an online critique group, and organizing twice-yearly conferences for the Wisconsin Fellowship of Poets.

After a year and a half of writing pretty much nothing but abecedarians, one day I found myself amazed to be done and began decompressing from the mental stress of a prolonged period of intense creative activity. For a week, my head felt lighter.

The poems in this book are presented in their order of composition, except "Bestiary." It and "Gilgamesh Tomb Found in Iraq" were both written eight years after the other poems, when I briefly returned to the form in 2016.

Michael Kriesel
Wausau, Wisconsin
November 2017

[1] In *A Poet's Glossary*, published by Houghton Mifflin Harcourt in 2014, Edward Hirsch writes, "Karl Elder's *Gilgamesh at the Bellagio* (2007) contains two sequences of fifty-two ten-syllable lines: the first series, 'Mead,' consists of twenty-six abecedarians, the second series, 'Z Ain't Just for Zabecedarium,' runs backward through the alphabet twenty-six times."

BESTIARY

A beast can't destroy everything.
Fame, glory, holiness insist.
Jealous, killing lust means nothing
once people quit raping & stealing.
Then, under Venus
we experience Yahweh's zodiac.

I. SINGLES

A MODERN GRIMOIRE

Astral gnome of doom, protect us.
Balance in all things. As above, so below.
Chant daily. Chant each morning. Chant when bored, or driving.
Demons surround us. Turn your back to them when summoning.
Earth, air,
fire, water.
God and the Kingdom of
Heaven are in you.
It's important to keep a daily
journal of dreams and visions, insights, intuitions.
Karma can't touch the wind.
Love is the law. Love under will.
Magic is causing change in conformity with will.
Numerology is contemplation
of the world's permutations.
PAY ATTENTION!
Qabbalah's a living religion. Each of us brings something to it.
Remember, your
soul's a muscle, too.
Two toads on a teeter-totter. Greed and sloth in balance.
UFOs are visitations from the fairy realm.
Visualize your own true
will and follow it to Heaven.
X is the true cross of man,
yet be not deceived by the
zombie Christ. None return from death.

ZEN AMEN

Zen. Zero. Zilch awaits all afterlives.
Yet somehow we can't imagine nothing.
X marks the spot. X must equal something.
Whether math or death, nothing must be named.
Vending machine? Why not? Let X be death's
ultramundane, unknowable chrome-legged
toy dispenser. Souls sucked in, toy coffins
spit out—unless that soul is on a string.
Remember Lazarus, recalled by Christ.
Qabbalistic texts agree how he was
pulled back from death like a coin on a string.
Oh, Jesus knew the secret would be safe—
no one who ever comes back recalls much,
mostly since there's nothing to remember.
Laugh if you want. It's good for the soul—though
killed, hope resurrects like dandelions.
Jesus knew all this. Still, he was right. We're
immortal, since mind can't survive its end.
How do I know all this? Easy. I died.
God wasn't there and neither was I that
first time in Madison, Wisconsin one
evening as I was leaning against a
dull red brick wall, chanting. And then I was
chanting, leaning against a red brick wall.
But there was a gap, and in my hand was
a toy coffin. Can I get an Amen?

HEAVEN'S NAIL

Zigzag hurled eternally by bearded
Yahweh, piercing VII heavens, binding
X realms, connecting, galvanizing the
whole universe, the Tree of Life, arbor
vitae, thus allowing highest heaven's
undifferentiated potential,
that clear cosmic Cool Whip called Kether to
sizzle down and manifest its will in
realms material. Dispersion's raven
quits its non-perch. Inflating, a bubble
pushes chaos into the abyss and
our brief universe of order exists.
Now I strike. Creation guide my hand. Remember, it's forever, what we do—this
light dressed as a nail. The hammer. The wood.
Keep it all focused—then release the act.
Just creating recreates the first act.
In the beginning, God's a carpenter.
Heaven's nail is driven through descending
globes grown denser until at last matter
finally carries Heaven's spark in it.
Even river stones have light inside them.
Dressed in dirt to know reunion's joy, light
converses with a tongue of hummingbirds,
blue whales—icebergs' discourse aimed at chaos,
all actions argument against abyss.

MIDDLE PILLAR

Zoroaster started it—good, evil,
Yahweh and the abyss eternally
x-ing swords. Pawns advanced, sacrificed. Pawns
with souls. Like God, our free will thwarted by
various circumstances. Anything
under the sun, really: sex, poverty,
tyranny, our towers falling on us—
stone swords broken against the blue heavens,
reptiles bequeathing petroleum, earth-
quakes, floods, war, that hole in the sky melting
polar ice caps. Perhaps what we need is
one good king or one big om to calm our
nerves' babbling snowy noise of nothingness.
Meditate. Maybe it's not too late to
lose your life along with everything that's
keeping you from your higher self. Maybe
just in time we could all Jesus ourselves
into what we really mean, making the
hanged man's sacrifice—that nameless, blinded
god swinging like a traffic light above
First and Main, staring down each golden dawn,
every sunset in its scorched orange eye,
dancing on nothing and on everything,
center pole in Creation's circus tent,
balancing act between Heaven and the
abyss, marrying light and nothingness.

CUP OF AIR

Zipping around the feeder, one drops dead,
yanked from air by time and sugar water.
X-rays might show a blown heart. I'm at the
window when it happens. I get a stick,
v-shaped at one end. A roll of duct tape.
Upon these heavens, my burnt offering.
The barbeque sizzles, gas at full blast.
Smoke rises from a ruby hummingbird,
redolent of flower nectar. I laugh,
quaff a breath, flagon of fumes, cup of air,
perfumed. Of course, it smells like chicken. The
odor spreads, permeating the entire
neighborhood, as I invoke the planet
Mercury, whose color vibrates orange,
like this burning orange thumb of a breast
killed by time, whose sign's an 8 on its side,
just as 8's the number of Mercury's
intelligences of the air. Chanting
Hebrew words of power, I invoke the
god Thoth, god of magic, writing, learning—
first scribe, whose wand and pen were one and same.
Enochian keys spill from my lips in
drabs and dribs, dribbling like rainbow syrup.
Certainly it's about power, control—
but mostly it's this reciprocity,
about possessing what possesses me.

New Age

Amethyst crystals for purifying.
Buddhist monks chant unobtrusively on
CD, vanilla candles freshening
drive-up window wisdom, enlightenment.
Elements unbalanced—mostly water's
flood of need. Dion Fortune's books useful.
Gargoyle statues. Semi-precious gems. Gnomes.
Healing energy masks no-fault foreplay.
Illusions mixed with spiritual truths.
Jewelry: moon earrings, amber pendants.
Ka: the name your soul went by in Egypt,
lives ago. Love is the law, under will.
Meditation group, Mondays. $15. The
needy flock. Om their groaning loneliness.
Owner wears a "Goddess Inside" T-shirt,
pushes pewter fairy figurines and
quartz in yellow, rose, smoke, orange and green.
Reiki massages in back. $70.
Sex magic manuals on sale. Celtic
tarot decks. Native American decks.
Unicorn figures multiply, warp the
very fabric of reality. Some
wizards in Toledo strike back, using
xylophones to raise storms in new age stores,
yoga studios—officially, freak
zephyrs are blamed, small indoor tornadoes.

ASCETIC VACATION

Zapped, my soul reboots. Buzzing recedes. I
Yin-yang my way back into consciousness.
X-ray vision (fading) gives a glimpse of
what must be eternal consciousness, devoid of distractions. God's vision, feasting
upon the world, eyes like twin eclipses.
Two eyes, two hands, two worlds, two feet meant to
straddle realities the way artists,
writers do, following life-long vision
quests, on vacation from themselves, the world.
Patience a negative quality, as
only the absence of distraction, as
nothing in itself. Desire slain, just to
more or less return as moderation—
leash in your hand, that was around your neck.
Kept in line. Good servant. Poor master. So
just enjoy the pretty girls, clean men, that
ice cream cone or beer. From here you can see
Heaven's blue void on a clear day, before
gorgeous skiffling clouds pull in like the fleet.
Fine. The world is Heaven manifest, and
emptiness alone can bear the burden
demanded by eternal consciousness.
Closest we approach down here is snow, or
blank fields of canvas, sheets of paper, all
awaiting vision's eye, senses abuzz.

XENOGENESIS

Zero hatches one from zip. Cosmic egg.
Yolk or chicken? Which came first? Both. At once.
Xenogenesis. Something from nothing.
White rabbit God pulls from a hat formed of
velvet darkness, though a second ago
you didn't see any hat, or God, for
that matter. Just darkness…then, a lance of
swirling atoms white as a gym sock that
randomly shows up overnight in a
quiet dryer. Goddamned if you know how.
Probably the same way houseflies appear
over winter between window panes, from
nothing, their lives black dots on a white beam.
Maybe they were right, those scholars with their
Latin, in the Middle Ages. How life
keeps rising from nothing. Worms form from soil,
just as fruit is made of sunlight, water,
in the same way that our lives are simply
handed to us, not unlike apports, those
gold coins dropping from the ceiling in old
Fate magazine articles, the work of
evil magicians or their familiar
demons, maybe. But I digress. I mean
can such things be? Showers of frogs, lasting
but a minute. Long enough to shake us,
and short enough to deny afterwards.

ZONE OF LIGHT

As I chant, my nervous system changes.
Beginning to paint, I'm possessed by light.
Colors hypnotize me, vibrate like red
dancing with green. I paint a black tree, limbs
everywhere coil in octopoidal scrolls.
Fat trunk. Small metal triangles for leaves—
glazier's points, spray-painted, glued to branches.
Hard to see against dark-blue poster board,
it flickers like the forest does at dusk,
just at the edge of visibility.
Kaleidoscopic watercolors bleed
light on panes of glass I hang in windows.
Meanwhile I'm beginning to see auras.
Nothing too dramatic. Just transparent
outlines around people. Muddy sheaths on
power lines and phone lines. It's a little
queer, but I get used to it. My friend Ben
rides Amtrak three days from Wisconsin to
Seattle to see me. We take in a
traveling Edward Hopper collection
uptown. In the last room, I almost get
vertigo. I'm inside a gold tunnel.
Waves of yellow. Huge canvas of a train
x-ing the plains at sunset. Two million
years of human evolution bought this
zone of light I linger in, long sunset.

Abbey Road

Apperception. Knowledge tattooed on my
brain. Like knowing my left hand's there, or time's
contemporaneous, with everything
demanding God's attention all at once,
every bill falling due now. No credit
for the lord of time who floats above the
grooves of linear experience. Old
hippies remember Abbey Road, Side 2.
In grooves we live, forced forward. In dreams we
jump the vinyl wall, travel astrally.
Kept in line by time. The only way we
learn down here. The perfect training tool. Time
merely measuring matter in motion.
No matter, no time. Just eternity's
ocean, and consciousness, attaining to
pure light's height, looking down on its record,
cued to every note at once. Then, a burst.
Release. We become lighthouses on a
shore with no sand or water, one at a
time. A light for others to steer towards,
until we're all light. Eternity's not
very long. A winter walk. A movie
where you're frozen between frames, like slides. You
exit, enter doorways in the air as
you balance on emptiness, between fields,
zippers jingling a second, stepping through.

TAROT

Zenora's crystal ball haunts me for days—
yellow quartz dragon's eye. At home I go
x-eyed trying to scry, but lack the knack.
What if I'm precognitively impaired?
Veil unrent, I make a magic mirror.
Undo the silver with a razor blade,
then spray-paint one side black. Moon face swims, dim.
Stares back, clueless. Tarot cards yield better
results. I obsess. Five readings a day.
Quit the present to pursue the future.
Pretty much the Fool, walking blindfolded
on the edge of a cliff—but flush with luck.
Never in danger—God's finger. I start
making my own cards, personalize fate.
Laminate each one. A card a day. The
kings have foil crowns. I have a great time with
judgment day—neon zombies rise from graves.
I make up a card: the outline of a
handprint. It stands for a life's potential.
Gradually fills with time, choices, acts.
Full, the hand vanishes. Leaves the card blank.
Each reading I shuffle in a trance, like
drunken poker—cards spread in a Celtic
cross, proving subatomic theory, where-
by consciousness affects what it observes:
a paper mirror, helping us reflect.

TETRAGRAMMATON

Automatically Binah appears,
black sea of time, whenever I see a
crow. Trios of crows tumble by, the sky
dark-gray as breakers on Lake Michigan,
even as Binah's the third sphere in that
filing cabinet called the Tree of Life,
God's blueprint for the universe. Ten realms
holding everything, ruled by the planets.
In Binah's case, Saturn. Its metal, lead—
just like the sky. Crows belong to Saturn.
Keep on going until everywhere you
look there's some kind of connection. Did I
mention it's the sphere of understanding?
Numerology comes later. First the
old woman touches you. Dark mother whose
perfume is the churchy smell of myrrh. Crone
queen who bestows the vision of sorrow,
rightful understanding of creation,
space as its receptacle. The world her
tarot card. The universe spent, complete.
Undiminished silence. Aspect of the
Virgin Mary. Hebrew letter tau, cross.
World as Tetragrammaton, God's true name,
exhausted and reborn as us, his seed.
Yes, it's an Easter egg hunt, seeking from
zenith to pit these pieces of our name.

CELL

Zero to my name. A mattress draped in
yellow morning light, an old white sink. 8
x 10 room. Cube of time I rent. $110
w/heat included. Old radiator.
Vows of mild poverty, celibacy
undertaken for the great work's sake. I
take a magical name: *Heaven's Nail*. The
Essenes would understand, long dead. Still more
real than many living dead. I study
Qabbalah and the Tree of Life each day.
Pump iron. See my soul's a muscle too.
Offer my life to my higher self. That
nameless angel's conversation saves me.
My own true will slowly possesses me.
Light feeds me like a tree. For three years I
keep this up. Inch back from the abyss. Spend
just such inheritance I left myself.
I still drink. No saint. But serve another,
higher creativity than just lust.
God may be a ladder we invent to
further reach. So what? Faith and magic work.
Either way, this life's a gift. Not mine. A
dance on air, like flame. A sacrifice. I
chant until I lose my name, nothing left
but this: my soul's ability to love
again, against the world's impermanence.

ORIGINAL SIN

Angels battle chaos demons, the war
between Hell and Heaven just beginning,
Christ still a corporal. Hitler too. All
depends on where you're standing. Everything
ends in a stalemate eleven seconds
from Lucifer's first swing at the old man.
God gets a shiner. Michael steps in. Bee-
hive of light tearing itself apart in
interstellar indigo. Not over.
Just the fact we're all here, from Cain on down,
killing each other over religion
leaves little doubt the war's still going on.
Most likely it spilled over into a
new arena. Angels with tails. Humans.
Openings between their legs for seeds of
prophets and holy warriors. Even
Qabbalists demonize their enemy.
Recruiting posters fill churches. You can
sign up at any synagogue or mosque.
Trivialize evil? Good? Wish I could!
Underestimate neither one's thirst for
vengeance. Meanwhile, disguised as all our small
wars, God's drags on. Satan mounts ad campaigns.
Xena the Warrior Princess straddles
Yggdrasil, her sword hacking its trunk, as
Zorro's sword tip zips Zarathustra's cheek.

Amber

Ant in amber. Its small sun for sale at
Bernie's Rock Shop, Madison, Wisconsin.
Cabbalist, I procure spell components.
Different gemstones for every planet,
each of the ten spheres of the Tree of Life.
Fossilized, dark trilobites wait on God's
grace to set them skittering again like
huge potato bugs, come future rapture.
I wonder if they'll eat the owner's cat?
Jupiter. Sapphire. Though any blue gem
keeps the vibrations harmonized. But I
love amber. Fossil pine pitch, twenty-five
million years old. Our Stone Age ancestors
knew it. Wore it while worshipping. It floats
on waves, washing up on shores. I wear a
pendant of amber. Midsummer. Golden
quartz at my feet. I enter the sphere of
rebirth: of Ra, Apollo, all the Christs.
Sphere of Tiferet, the sun. Clearing in
the woods behind the house. Noon. I offer
up false egos, petty fears to fire, light,
vampire crumbling in on myself, until
what's left is sure as bone, canine teeth. Dusk
exhumes me. I resurrect at the last
yellow moment from my bath of ashes.
Zircon sparks swarm like hornets from my eyes.

Blasphemy

Abomination blessed be. How at
birth the stars mark us. The beast, Aleister
Crowley, swore a mighty oath. Christ on toast!
Declared his will on Earth. Demonstrated
each man and every woman is a star.
Fuckery and genius wrapped in bullshit.
God walks in a church. Priest says believe in
Heaven or be damned to Hell forever.
"I do," God says, and she marries himself.
Juggler of realms, selves, the Rubik's Cube of
Kabbalistic truths, where men fish all their
lives on a heaven-blue sea—fishers of
men, masters every one of them. Once, in
North Africa, he summoned the demon
of the abyss into himself for its
power. Choronzon, the babbler. Crowley
quieted the demon for years through sheer,
raw force of will, but eventually,
still, the effort took its toll on the old
toad of Hell, who'd kick heroin, then start
up again to prove his will. Plus, all that
voltage ripping through him. Gradually
went mad, fat and old. Still, he did help map
Xanadu. I pound the bar with a fist.
Yell for a beer. A shot. A glass of cold
Zinfandel. Toast his holy blasphemy.

Essay in Numbers

Auschwitz. Rabbis put God on trial. Which side
broke the covenant? God. They still pray. The
commandant hears this. Smiles. Evil is the
devil's covenant with us. How else to
explain it? I'm fourteen. Standing in a
field when I sense a world behind the world.
Gematria (g'mut'ree'ah) hovered,
hidden, just beyond my understanding.
In each Hebrew letter hides a number,
just like meat in a nutshell. God's shell game.
Kabbalists know under each shell something
lies. Robin's egg. Olive. Gold tooth. The world
makes more sense when seen as an essay in
numbers. Neptune's face in a mosaic.
Opals. Bones. Turds. All of them bricks in God's
pyramid, the world. Answer to this pop
quiz? The bigger the base, the higher it
rises. It's called the great work. We reach the
stars. Become pillars holding up Heaven.
There's a silence that follows learning this.
You might hear it as a ringing from the
vacuum of space. The music of the spheres?
Warning sign of a stroke? Maybe nervous
exhaustion? The Biblical approach of
Yahweh? Or just the alchemical buzzing of bees turning thistles to honey?

APPRENTICE

"A true apprenticeship lasts a lifetime,"
boasts the red matchbook cover. Four weeks of
correspondence courses later and I'm
dodging taxes with church status. I spew
eternal truths. Can marry couples in
fourteen states. In the mailing tube, a wand—
gopher wood, rolled up in the diploma.
"Himalayan masters deem you worthy,"
it says, "to share eternity's secrets."
Just like the government. A license to
kill, steal, obfuscate. Better than money,
love. I've got God on my side. I can cloud
minds with a word. Great at the singles bars.
Neat trick at the racetrack. I stop by the
office to empty my desk, pick up my
paycheck. People ask if I've lost weight. "Don't
quit," my boss implores. "Don't rob us of your
radiance." On my way out the door, his
secretary slips me her number. It's
thundering in the distance. The sky's blue.
Undone by a moment's compassion, I
veer to miss a squirrel—hit the neighbor's
wiener dog, right by the cemetery.
Xs for eyes. If Christ could, why can't I?
Yipping, he bounds off. Then I see the first
zombies approaching. My wand shoots daisies.

Oil of Abramelin

Anoint the crown chakra (top of head) first.
Brow next, where it burns slightly, more from the
cinnamon oil than from enlightenment.
Divine spark of my higher self that I'll
eventually be reunited
fully with. That's what the oil represents.
Grace. Aleister Crowley's version's called the
"holy oil of aspiration." Light gold,
it is derived from the formula for
Jewish holy oil. Sacrament of self.
Kept in the altar when it's not in use.
Light cinnamon smell. Plus olive oil and
myrrh. Galangal root (like ginger). I learn
new smells. Basil sharpens concentration.
Oils and incenses. I experience
phantosmia on a winter walk—air
queerly rich with lilacs. Then, the bathroom
rank with cheap aftershave. Angels, demons
sending me their regards? Usually
these phantom odors arise during the
unpleasant part of an exorcism—
vomit, feces, rotting flesh and sulfur.
"Wake up! Smell the coffee!" my higher self
exhorts, exasperated. I'm trying.
Yet part of me rolls over, catches more
Zs. Dreams of amaretto, hazelnut.

KARMA BUNKER

Zillionth of a second after I'm in—
yelling. Pounding on the door. Saint Francis
Xavier says he was here first. Needed
wafers. Just stepped out for a minute. "The
Virgin Mary will forgive your sins if
you let me in!" Bliss dangles on a string.
The Lesser Banishing Ritual With
Silver Star serves to get rid of him. I
really just want to be left alone. Peace.
Quiet. Solitude. The doorknob rattles.
"Possession's nine-tenths of the law!" I shout.
Ommm. I chant, trying to stay calm. Focused.
"No one wants you here!" I yell. Then I hear
mumbling. Someone stumbles through bad Latin.
Lilac incense pours under the door. "You're
killing me!" I cry. "O bleeding feet of
Jesus!" I'd like a nap. A walk. Then an
ice cream cone, maybe. You can't get those in
Hell, though it's cold enough there to freeze ice,
God forbid. I sigh, crack a window and
fart corpse gas. Then I make the old woman,
Eunice, squeal like a pig—like her lover's
dick used to, by the lake in his beat-up
car sixty years ago. Time for the old
battle of wills. The room exhales. Time runs
ahead, black dog, and all the blue paint peels.

Loop in a Field

And again, everything rewinds and I'm
banishing the elements in a small
clearing in the woods behind an old farm,
drawing pentagrams in the air with an
elm wand. They shimmer like heat waves, briefly.
Four rocks painted silver form a circle,
glitter in the weeds. North. South. East. West. Each
has a symbol. Sun. Moon. Eye. Crow. Next thing
I'm above the trees, looking down on me
just like a hawk, paused between lightning bolt
kills. Nail driven into the sky. Then down.
Looking up at blue vertigo. I laugh.
Make the sign for earth, chanting one of God's
names, clearing all the sluggish energy
out of the area. I summon fresh
powers of fire, earth, air, water. There's a
quiet buzzing in my chest. Drowsy wasp.
Refocusing, I notice skinny souls,
see a stand of birches. They're summoning
the snow. It's suddenly December. I'm
under gray clouds. Then they melt in greenish
violet light that comes before a storm.
Winter's sickle, summer's muscle mingle
ecstasies. Light starts to clot in the leaves.
Yellow watercolors spread. Seasons whiz-
zing by. Clouds race. The sky's fast-forwarding.

PLANETS IN US

Zodiac of possibilities I'm
young enough to entertain—find my own
Excalibur, given the right lady
with the right lake. I prepare to contact
Venus via ritual, a good week's
undertaking. White roses. Rose perfume.
The white cat. Emerald. Green robe. I paint
symbols. Script everything. Memorize and
rehearse until it's automatic. Then
quit. Take a day off. Meditate. Pray. Fast.
Planetary forces correspond with
ones in our own psychic makeup. Goddess
Nike, victory in me. I need be
my own Merlin. My own Vivian, too—
Lady of the Lake. Go forth in myself.
Kill what needs killing. Enforce the king's will,
justice, on self's wilderness. Cultivate
in my soul a kind of park. Inculcate
harmony between the forces in me.
Gods and monsters, myths and archetypes called
forth full force. Then pruned back, balanced, until
eventually nothing stands between
destiny and me. The stars' roulette wheel
calmly waits, as does selfhood's throne—true will.
But first I have to slay the slayer, the
astral gnome of doom, my own last tulpa.

Astral Projection

Zooming the astral plane, quick as a thought
you're in Tibet—then Bangor, Maine. Your soul
exits your body like a sneeze, wanders
weightless, fleck of ectoplasm, your eyes
vacant, vulnerable to possession.
Ugly things happen sometimes in magic.
There's risk of tulpas: malignant, mindless
spirits formed by the subconscious. Like that
rascally rabbit, Bugs Bunny. Really
quite unrestrained when met with astrally.
Psychotic, like all cartoon characters.
Of course he has a carrot. And a knife.
Now on the surface the astral plane's not
much different than a dream. But symbols
live there. Archetypes and lower beings.
Kali's there. The Grail. Bigfoot. Poltergeists.
Just about anything man (or one man)
invests with psychic energy. More than
has ever existed here on Earth is
gathered there, waiting for material
form. A world of dreams awaits birth. The more
experienced use Kabbalah to help
distinguish between "real" symbols and what
can be recognized as self-delusion.
But that crazy rabbit with the steak knife?
Avoid him. Or wake up craving carrots.

PRINCE OF TREES

Asparagus dissolves in a cloud of
bright citrine. Some days I bike twenty miles,
chanting while balancing on tires thin and
dark as a tree's growth rings. Been celibate
eleven years. Celibate as trees. Just
for practical reasons, mostly. It helped
give me a fighting chance to change. Became
habit, which is what a lot of magic
is—new pathways of thought, action. It takes
just twenty-eight days to form a habit.
Kind of like the man in the moon helps. I
labor to achieve dominion over
me—ex-slut in a sailor suit in my
Navy days. Living up north, fixing Dad's
old place. I lift weights. Cut brush. A self-crowned
prince of trees selling firewood to tourists.
Quit journalism. Part-time janitor
right down the road. Elementary school.
Suddenly I'm forty. Card trick done with
these colored leaves, autumn keeps repeating
until time is so much paper to me.
Verily—to know, dare, keep silent. The
wise often hide, glad that people don't have
x-ray sight. Most burn witches in their hearts.
Yes. Each day's another brick in my life's
ziggurat, rising in Wisconsin's heart.

WISCONSIN PYRAMID

African swamps still harbor dinosaurs—
brontosaurs and triceratops, mostly.
Cryptozoologists cite coelacanths,
deep-sea stragglers left from the Cretaceous
Era. Once believed extinct, they argue
for survival of other species thought
gobbled by time. The lack of facts doesn't
hinder speculation, you'll find, on the
internet. Bloggers and websites connect
just about everything from Jesus to
KFC's secret recipe to the
lost tribes of Israel to the Loch Ness
monster. One popular theory places
Nessie on that grassy knoll in Dallas.
Only how'd it pull the trigger with those
prehistoric flippers? First answer that
question. Then work your way back until the
rest all falls into place. The truth holds still
sometimes long enough for us to capture
that backwards glance as Bigfoot disappears,
UFO waiting nearby. I've come to
view the truth much like that pyramid in
Wisconsin at the bottom of a lake.
Exactly why it's there a mystery,
yet so far no one's explored this sunken
ziggurat sitting right in front of us.

ALPHA

Xeroxed, my poems ride along in back.
You never know when the house'll burn down.
Exorcising one demon frees me to
worry about another. Wavy, a
vee of geese sends me to the bathroom. Still
unexpired, that hundred-dollar box of
Tamiflu. Three weeks I spent brooding last
summer about bird flu. My bipolar
roller coaster ride has taught me one thing—
quit pretending fate's impersonal. I
perceive Heaven's hand each day. Placebo
or not, it keeps me functioning. Alive.
Nuttiness aside, there's this—it teaches
me to care, and not to care. I learn to
love with a dispassionate compassion,
keep feeding my heart to the wind till there's
just enough left to appreciate things.
It's 60 degrees and the snow's in a
hurry, braiding the ditches with rivers.
Green patches burn through the snow here and there,
fresh and green as the world's early birthdays.
Even the empty beer can sailing past
dazzles me as I sit watching on the
cement steps. The sun hits it just right. It
blazes, and the world's unborn in brightness,
all things held again in one white second.

WHERE LIGHT GOES

Zombie Christ rises like a B-movie.
Yet be not deceived. None return from death.
X is the true cross of man, marks the spot
where light goes, leaving images behind.
Vivid an instant. Gone but permanent.
Understand, like light, we die. Otherwise
time would stop. We'd all still be in Egypt,
still building pyramids, still watching the
river of snakes swimming the dress of that
cute Egyptian girl dicing onions, a
paring knife in her hand. My eyes are wet
on waking, face numb from loss. Her face still
no less real than mine. Or that pair of eyes—
magician's eyes—from fifteen years ago.
Lord of Illusions, The Great Sandini
knifed my soul, staring from a 10-foot-tall,
jet-black poster. An ephemera shop
in Pike Place Market. Like twin eclipses
his eyes burned through the decades between us,
glowed like fire opals. Grew white-hot as road
flares. Gazed on the essential dead, bricks in
ethereal pyramids. Agnostic,
Dad gets a Christian burial. Some small
comfort to Mom. We drive through sloppy snow.
Below, toads hibernate. And I curse time's
architect for being right, forever.

Hollow Earth

Amazing. Another world emerges,
brooding behind the usual headlines.
Cow mutilations. Crop circles. The floor
drops out from under me like the hollow
earth's Antarctic entrance, where top Nazis
fled with A. Hitler after World War Two.
Global warming and rising gas prices
have a lot less meaning in a world with-
in a world. The Incas hid their empire's
jewels and gold from Conquistadors and
kindly Pizzaro in secret tunnels
left by Atlanteans. They honeycomb
much of South America, part of a
network connecting every continent
on the planet. UFOs and our own
present-day military use them, ac-
cused by some of conducting genetic
research experiments on abductees.
Subterranean cities abandoned
thousands of years ago have now become
underground torture chambers beneath our
very feet. Miles below us, another
world undermines our lives. Paranoid? Yes.
X doesn't always mark treasure on maps.
Yet despite the horror, I follow my
zeal—gold thread I clutch in this labyrinth.

AKASHIC RECORDS

Zenobia, Palmyra's queen, fought Rome—
yet each single second of her life still
exists. Thoughts. Events. Her responses. Face
wet from tears, heat. Her actions and words still
vibrating in the ether, viewable
under certain conditions by mystics,
those who attune themselves by various
spiritual disciplines like yoga,
ritual magic, different ways of
quieting the mind and attaining the
pre-conscious state needed for witnessing
of the Akashic records. The prophet
Nostradamus read them. Edgar Cayce's
medical readings were based on the past
lives of his patients sometimes, stored in a
kind of Smithsonian of the soul, a
Jungian collective unconsciousness,
including all haiku yet to be felt.
Harp with an infinity of strings plucked.
God's living memory. Prehistoric
ferns inch open. All the tribes of frogs and
every future history preserved, a
diary of everybody, ever.
Complete set of encyclopedia
bound several billion years before an
aardvark or zebra even existed.

SIDEREAL PENDULUM

Architect Ludwig Straniak finds a
battleship with a pendulum and sea
charts, though its location's a secret. Il
Duce's found the same way, held prisoner
east of Rome, sprung by SS commandos.
From World War Two Germany we jump to
Great Britain, the nineteen-seventies. In
his retirement, one Thomas Charles Lethbridge
investigates pendulum dowsing and,
just like others before him, this former
keeper of antiquities at Cambridge
learns you can find almost anything by
merely dangling a crystal on a string.
Not unlike using an L-shaped brass rod
or Y-shaped hazel twig to find water.
People have dowsed for fifty centuries.
Quartz and flint, Lethbridge found, have vibration
rates that cause a fifteen-and-a-half inch
string to respond. Ideas, emotions,
thoughts and colors trigger reactions too.
Up to forty: iron, anger, death. A
void then, till one hundred forty, when the
whole thing repeats, just to the left. One could
extrapolate a second, phantom realm,
yet nothing damning. The existence of
z to the nth power realities.

Electronic Voice Phenomenon

Zeitgeist of no time or place, the voices
yell sometimes, though we don't hear. Maybe they
exist to haunt our tape recorders since
we only hear them in playback, hollow
voices drowned in static, when recording
undersea silences in empty rooms.
"Tom's here." Any self-respecting ghost or
soul would've dissolved in Heaven or Hell,
reincarnated years ago. Tom's mom
quietly cries. Falls in love with her grief,
playing the message every day for weeks.
Or is it pareidolia? The human
need to find a pattern, hear words where there's
merely noise. See faces in clouds or on
late night, snowy TV screens. "I want to
kill you all!" Maybe they're not our loved ones.
Just Hell's disinformation campaign. One
in twelve messages openly hostile.
Hoax? The researcher's own thoughts, projected?
"God. We all turn here." Some bring recordings
for presentation at conventions of
EVP researchers. "What about trans-
dimensional beings?" a voice asks. "You
can't deny there's something," says another.
"But what? My money's on fragments of the
Akashic records. Just echoes, like ghosts."

SERPENT MOUND

Amateur occult investigator
by sixteen, my first field trip is in a
Chevy Nova with a friend who has his
driver's license. Fourth of July weekend.
East of Cincinnati we learn map skills,
find thirteen hundred feet of serpent, its
green length a grassy wave frozen five feet
high, tail spiraling down into nothing,
island of a hill that could be the world
just beyond gaping jaws. Or another
kind of myth, reversed. A giant worm de-
livering the world in birth. Serpent's tail
morphs into a worm's head circling up from
nothing. It's enough to make you dizzy,
open can of beer aside. The native
people shaped their heads with boards. Flat as snakes.
Quakes, minor, occur. The mound's on a cliff,
raised by ancient violence underground.
Standing on the snake's head, facing Eden,
the wind picks up and the earth seems to move,
undulating briefly. The whole trip's a
vertigo postcard in my head. Blurred hours
winding our way home through Ohio hills,
x-country, stopping at small-town bars. Drunk,
young geek, I babble on divination—
zoomancy—as Holsteins moo the future.

Book of Wonders

Zygomancy: divination with weights.
You can tell the future with a book, too—
examine random passages for clues.
Weighing something against the Bible de-
veloped this way. Waiting in line, I zone
until tabloid headlines coalesce into a page of fortune cookie fortunes
shimmering with possibility. I
read between the lines, see hidden meanings,
quasar-bright, in "DNA scientists
prove hen was once T-Rex." Giant drumsticks
on *The Flintstones* make sense. Maybe you do
need a hotdog cart in a graveyard at
midnight in order to catch a ghost, just
like on *Scooby-Doo.* Maybe someday some
kind of small primate, our descendant, will
jump in the trees while giant mosquitoes
invent TV sets that can watch the past.
H.P. Lovecraft and H.P. Blavatsky
gave us pieces of the puzzle. The world's
filled with common miracles, besides what
each imagination knows. Go ahead,
draw connections until the ink runs out.
Cut yourself on your own argument's edge.
But in the end, take it on faith. It's all
about awe—this world's sheer weight of wonder.

DITCH GODDESS

A bird road follows the ditch's ripe straw-
berries, small as candy hearts. (Remember
chalk yellow, sea green, Pepto-Bismol pink?)
Ditch Goddess, I watch cattails' slow motion
explosions last for days. You've been one less
failure for me. These pines would only be
green lines without you. Windy grass whips me
home past summer's muscle and winter's bone.
In your absence, lady, snow itself is
just an absence, instead of these light fields'
keen vision of a personal heaven.
Lady of thistle crowns, periwinkle
mixes with dusk and I blink. Sometimes it's
not what we are, but what we're not. You've been
one less failure of mine. Never lovers.
Pedestals get in the way. Plus my heart
quarrels like blackbirds. A white screen door slaps.
Red chevrons arrowing all directions
scatter into the unfinished fall heat.
The sky's a navy blue abyss. I walk
under stars I don't believe in. Stars that
veer down from the hills until the lake is
white with them. I'd be totally alone
except my heart's a lake that holds the moon.
You're here. I dream myself awake. Cattails'
zodiac of fluff dances on nothing.

II.   DOUBLES

Fungi from Yuggoth

Zemo, Hell's Baron, face always ablaze.
Yellow flames licking his head finally
extinguished. Decapitation. An ax
wielded by Doctor Strange, archmage. One blow.
Vital lesson comics taught me at twelve:
ugly things occur in the occult. You
try a spell anyway. Nothing, at first.
Still, the back of the neck knows better, as
random acts begin. Lightning rod, the air
quiets all around me. A Suzy Q
plops on the table at lunch. I look up.
Overhead, a hole in the air leads to
nowhere. I long for normalcy's return.
Mechanistic universe. Start to om.
Lovecraftian blue tentacles plug all
kitchen sink drains. Strangle the cat. Attack
just as I'm flushing a stale PBJ.
It's enough to make you pray. Almost. I
hear the abyss howl behind the wall. Tough
guy, I make a deal with some crabs that wing
freely across the interstellar gulf,
Earth to Yuggoth in two days. My brain's here,
dangling from a giant claw, in a sealed
can with speakers, lens, though I can't lip sync—
but better the devil you know—like Bob,
a great guy, my ride across the void's sea.

PHILOSOPHER'S STONE

Alchemy begins and ends with man. A
breath of light, phosphorus discovered. Lab
chemistry for the poet and mystic.
"Dissolve and combine." Add the grace of God.
Extract color, weight, shape, until you have
first matter. Then add the qualities of
gold. King Midas, with a better ending.
Heaven in you. Heresy, to the church.
Integrating personality, I
juggle animal, mineral and veg.
Keep my balance. Undertake the great work.
Lead into silver, then into gold. All
metals keep on growing in the earth's womb,
nurtured by their planets' influence. Tin
of Jupiter. Iron, Mars. Copper to
pure gold evolves by Venus' grace. Some stop.
Quit short of perfection. A bit risqué—
red daughter weds crowned king. Their gentle fire
sexy metallurgy. Self-marriage, this
transmutation of dross into bliss. That
universe within/without an egg you
vow to love, dressed in obscure symbols of
wolf, dragon, unicorn. The sun's yellow
explosion fills each second. Tantric sex.
Yet continuing. The world a holy
Zen stone dissolving in my soul's gold fizz.

ESCHATOLOGY

Zohar, book of splendor, posits God's jizz.
Yanked back and everything's biography
x-ed out, creation collapses. Last lux
winks out. Stars drop. Light bulbs pop. Eyeballs blow.
Void rushing, Leviathan rides last wave.
Undoubtedly the world has to end. You
take your pick. Asteroid. Fire. Zombies. But
so what? Whether whiz-bang or whimper, it's
really academic. Scientists are
queued behind global warming these days. Bask
perhaps in the sun before our time's up,
ozone gone. Get drunk. Call in sick. Or go
nuts worrying. We still have to go on.
Maybe the future does give today some
larger meaning. For now the Ferris wheel
keeps spinning—the only show in town. Like
judgment's wheel, we all ride it. Hold your fudges-
icle or drop it on someone's head. I
hand my own heart to Anubis to weigh
against a feather, light as light, begging
forgiveness in exchange for my belief.
Egyptian gods will do until I wake.
Doomsday makes any afterlife look good.
Coffee. A shower. Soon I'm a stoic.
Back to normal again. Just glad to be
alive and feeling good and here today.

What's Missing

Zodiac of falling milkweed fuzz, froze.
"Yes," I mutter, half hypnotized by sky,
x-eyed. The word's puff dissolves in white flux.
Will flaps off in the form of a white crow.
Vertigo. I don't feel the cold. Must have
undertaken this prior to birth. You
try to be the change you want to see, but
sometimes forget what you meant, back in Earth's
realm, fresh from Heaven's dream, on whatever
quest seemed clear and worthwhile. The soul goes back-
packing, in search of what's missing. I strap
on familiar shackles of muscle. Go
naked to the world. Leave fields of light in
my subconscious, that memory gone dim,
lit up by my nerves' neon carnival.
Keep fucking up. Booze almost takes me back.
Justify whatever I do. Steal. Fudge,
if it's in my own interest. Then I
have an epiphany because the ache
gnawing at me grows until there's nothing,
finally. I can't even feel my grief.
Evening. Popcorn. I'm watching a police
drama on TV. Some poor soul is dead,
chalk outline left like an ectoplasmic
body. It hits me. I begin to grab
at absences I meant to take away.

WHITE CROW

"Zzz." Static. July, and I'm feeling laz-
y. Crows call, far above me. Trinity
excreta. Feathered turds, circling. My ex-
wife's telling me I'm full of shit. One crow
veers off from the other two. We both have
unresolved issues we need to work thru.
The cell phone grows heavy in the sun's heat.
"Scatology's my field!" I quip. But she's
right. Still, I give it one last try. "There are
Qabbalistic grimoires on the great work
postulating the soul progresses upon the Tree of Life via forms of o-
nanism," I obfuscate. On the phone,
my soul says I need an enema. I'm
losing the signal, so I jab redial.
"Kaw." One crow is white now. The others black.
Just then, my ex picks up. "Don't hang up, Madge!
I…I can change. Each saint has a past." I
hear what sounds like a crow on the line. "Ah…
goddamn it!" The wind picks up. More cawing.
Flapping. Crows tumble, shingles from Hell's roof.
Each sinner has a future, Oscar Wilde
declared. "I can't believe we were married!"
caws a harsh voice in my ear. I panic,
begin petitioning the wind. I jab
at the air as a white crow soars away.

DEUS EX MACHINA

Air opens. There's a hole. Ozone. A buzz.
Big as a kitchen table, this pinky
comes poking through. Stops halfway. Wiggles. Ex-
Deus. God checks our temperature. How
else explain it? That buzz, like the dream of
free power that Tesla had, broadcast thru
giant towers. An electric air that
hums my bones until my vision becomes
incredibly sharp. The finger's whorls are
jutting lines in the sand Zen masters rake,
keeping meditation gardens. I slip
loose from the cuffs of my wrists, letting go
much like Houdini at death. A knife thrown,
neatly slicing an apple above some
orange-bikini-clad assistant. Hole
popping shut behind my soul/mind, I'm stuck.
Quicksand made of light. I can't even J-
run or walk. No legs. Just thought. The pinki'
s gone. So is everything else. A couch,
two pillows would be nice. But there's nothing,
unless imagination counts. Bright fluff.
Vacuum of fluorescent light. White silence.
Where am I? Heaven's roof? Inside of God?
Existential Hell? Stay calm. Don't panic
yet, I tell myself. Stretch out. Maybe grab
zzz's. I wonder if God started this way.

ATHEIST HEAVEN

A whale of stars swallows me. Fly, I buzz,
backstroking in milk, but don't get any
closer to a person, place, thing. This sucks
dead clowns. I drown in light. Revive. Somehow,
eons later, I stand by an act of
faith on numb legs, lost in gobs of tofu.
Gradually, sky breathes. Piles form of that
heavenly matter sought by alchemists.
I scoop some up with my new hands, wonder
just where it comes from—part solid, part liq.
Kind of sticky. Bit warm. Maybe it simply pops up from nothing. I make a snowman. Throwing a snowball, whisper, "Raven."
Now a raven flies away—croaking, grim
offering to silence. I think a while.
"Paul," I order the snowman, "Get to work."
Quickly he rolls away. I say "O.J."
Rearranging light to suit my taste, I
slurp down an orange smoothie. Make a wish.
Twin albino willows. A hammock hung
underneath. But soon I hit the ground. Laugh.
Vacuum's restored again. Heaven's empty.
Why am I still here then? I wish real hard,
exasperated. Castle with AC.
Yet it dissolves like wet sand. Give up, ab-
solved of all desire. Wait to fade away.

THE FALL

Adam in Heaven. Names create. I say
"buff abs"—instant six-pack. But all my flab
comes back quick as sin. Crispy KFC
dissolves like cotton candy in rain, and
every fucking hour I'm hungry. Chinese
food? Same thing. Everything here's so much fluff.
Gobs of unmanifest potential. Hog
Heaven for minimalists. I call forth
ink. Peacock feather. Watch the letter I
just wrote turn invisible. What fog cage
keeps me here? Habit's rut? Desire grown lack-
luster? Lust's afterlife? Or is my will
meager, too weak to sculpt creation from
nothing, unable to focus, maintain
objects continuously? A big toe
pops out of nowhere, a flourish of harp.
Quickly I turn, drop my running critique.
Run instead through cosmic Cool Whip. Flames roar,
shooting from the toe. It's big as a bus.
Two angels with swords help give me the boot.
Unable to fill God's shoes, my new view,
virtue of falling from grace, is one of
wonder—stars blur, angels point and laugh. How
exactly do I breathe in space? Some hex
Yahweh stuck me with? I cross the black abyss, toward a blue world I recognize.

Forgetting Heaven

"Zzz-zz!" Wake myself snoring. A blue jay
yells at me. Bizarre pizza dreams fade. Bob
explained they're caused by spices. Agnostic,
was I in a Twinkie? My host/ess God?
Viscous whiteness. Then I swoop down kite-like,
unborn. Enter the back of the head of
the man who will father me. Like watching
some movie I'm in. Cloud gazing, I laugh,
remember Heaven's warm whiteout. My I.
Q. drops. I'm so hung over. Damn blue jay
piercing my brain—tiny dinosaur shriek.
On Mom's card table there'd be a puzzle.
Now there are several at the same time:
maples' orange eulogies. Beach. Mountain.
Like poet, sailor, witch: a guy could go
krazy separating pieces. Give up
jigsaw memories. Is that BBQ
I smell? Bob must be up. The guy's a bear.
He knew me in the Aleutian Islands.
Gunner's Mate. Last night we closed the Crow's Nest,
found ourselves towards dawn at Xanadu's
Exotic Dancers on Route 45.
Don't recall much. Heaven's a marshmallow?
Crows talking to me. A week in detox.
Buildings linked by tunnels. Blizzards. Navy
air base in Alaska. A girl named Liz.

NAVY WITCH

A ship's a hole steel punches in the sea.
But our ship? Future crater. Floating bomb
carrying fuel, named for a volcanic,
dormant Maui peak. We sat at pier's side
each night, Supply Center Oakland. The base
famous for its CO—the father of
god-of-rock Jim Morrison, "Lizard King."
Haze-gray paint covered everything. Our berth-
ing compartment held sixty guys. Young, bi
journalist, I'd stay at the Flying J
"kleen rooms" motel one night each payday week,
leave USS Haleakala. All
my shipmates but one thought a blonde, her name
Nora, waited at my cab ride's end, on
one of those vibrating beds you have to
plug quarters in. The truth? An envelope.
Q & A worksheets. Spells by mail. Antique
ritual knife cutting symbols in air.
Self-trinity of sailor, witch, queer—years
torpedoed, sunk, before I could admit
you three to me, myself, I. We're tabu.
Volanticas, Roman witches, some of
which were fed to volcanoes. I see how
exposure's constant threat warped. No phoenix,
yester-me survived and left the Navy.
Absolved with time my life absorbs its selves.

Teen Shaman

As above, so below. Marlboro haze
blues the room, torn screen window's heavenly
cerulean. Comix. Candles. Hot wax
dripped in water telling the future. However, I wouldn't drink it. My skull's cave
filled with words. Buried alive in Wausau
goddamn Wisconsin, a junior at East
High. Cutting off all my hair last Christmas,
I hung it on the tree. It grew. I swear.
Juvenile mystic, I can't be unique.
Kindred spirits must exist somewhere. Help.
Living in trailer. Mom works at Photo
Mart. Dad's gone. I re-create myself in
notebooks. Mimic crows. Ignore classmates—some
of whom avoid me in the halls. Not all.
Phys. ed and study hall I skip. Go drink.
Queens'll buy me tap beer sometimes at J.
R.'s bar, a few blocks up the alley. I
sleep on the bus ride home. Dream I'm in math.
They're all zombies, except one girl. Waking
up, there's drool on my shirt. Last stop. Sea of
verdancy. Cornfield. Trailer court. Sweet home
where I spin among stalks, a dervish whirled,
exhausted, lying in the dirt, epic
yet unbegun, dizzy with my life's ab-
surdities, freedom still a year away.

OFFICE DERVISH

After work we'd play computer games, slay
basilisks, dragons in the barracks. Bob
Cole and I were in the Navy. Office
dervish, he'd spin in his chair like a kid
each morning. Pour Pixy Stix in coffee
(fluorescent straws of colored sugar.) Quaff
gallons of the stuff. Lunch was a hot dog.
He was hairy as a hobbit, each patch
inspired in its own direction. I
just shook my head and laughed whenever Maj.
Krause told him, "Get a haircut after work!"
Little good crew cuts did against that whorl,
matter's DNA tornado no comb,
no gel could bend to its will, discipline,
organize in columns, lines, rows. No. Os
persist, persevere—atoms, planets, tops,
quantum marbles. Orbits often oblique
rather than mechanically round. Our
selves revolving too, past and future lives
tangled. I spin my chair. Chant. Catapult
unto a state of Bob—wall/window/blue
vinyl couch/bookcase bought at Goodwill. Love
waits at enlightenment's door, a pearl glow,
exactly what you'd hope the truth protects,
you and I older than our lives, those dizzy pearls spun around pain the world bestows.

Secret Women

Anchors on chiefs' and officers' hats blaze
bronze, gold. Fear holds us, though technically
seamen are Navy property. But sex?
Dismissed. Inspection done. Red stripes. White crow.
Each left sleeve flies one. Our navy blue wave
falls apart. First night in Honolulu.
Girls love us. Gays too. I'm nineteen. My white
hat gleams like a seagull under streetlights.
I kiss another sailor. Don't bother
justifying it. Part of its mystique.
Khaki conspiracy of fear. A lip
lock in a bar. It's payday. Tabasco
moon, where witches send secrets. Wisconsin:
no one recognizes me when I'm home
on leave. Rednecks tell faggot jokes. I smile.
"Purple Kool-Aid sea," I say. They nod. Drink.
Quietly I work. No UCMJ
ready to jail or discharge me. Nights I
summon secrets from the moon. Bits of ash.
Tiny rain of flakes from mirrors. Once begun, each secret summons another. Self
viewed in pieces. A broken vase. All me:
Witch. Sailor. Queer. My poetry unread
except by a few poets. Mosaic.
Y and X chromosomes balanced. Blowjob.
Zipper. Moon always broken on the sea.

SHEOL

Ash's memory of light and heat, these
broken shells, this plateau of shards, clay gray.
Crickets scratch a song from just themselves, lux
departed, withdrawn, long gone. The glass blow-
er's broken fishbowls still hold eels, volts of
flame snap, leftover sparks angels rescue,
guide back upstairs. It's one of those jobs that
harp-slingers live for, like leading lost souls
into light, salvaging slivers of star.
Just beginning, God applied too much torque,
Kabbalists claim. Saxophone not warmed up.
Lugubrious note left broken worlds. No
moans vibrate here, no contrite choir of sinners. Just echoes waiting for a sound. Dam
of memories burst, I recall a hell
peculiar to my youth, half in this bleak
Qliphoth, the Tree of Life's root, mired in sludge,
rest of me on Earth, all the lights on, bi-
sected, the walls between nights grown thin, moth
talc in the air. I'm drinking and writing.
Upholstering the windows, dozens of
vellumy moths, blank stamps that mail the house
while I write. Meanwhile in Hell, the crow I'd
exchanged bodies with gives a damnific
yawn. Time's up. As in youth, I'm just a dumb
zebra moth tattering limits, each day.

MINERAL KINGDOM

Angleworms as an abstract alphabet,
blacktop wet. Phone lines repeating blackbirds,
calling me. A corn-stubble field grows crows.
Dreaming of flight, I glide new roads. Driveway.
Engine block ticks down...frogs start up. Evening.
Frogs full blast. I light a firecracker's fuse.
Golden Lotus brand. Shoot my paper gun.
Hold off. Let them start again. This is how
I say my name tonight. Something else I'll
just say. The world's jammed with miracles. Just
kneel. Behold grass. Blue caves. A corn kernel's
light sings from one, tiny life dropped lightly,
maybe by a passing crow. It glows more
now as darkness rises like ground mist. Now
opalescent, gold gone, it oscillates.
Pale milk tooth, baby moon, it becomes pink
quartz and vibrates with all other quartzite.
Rib Mountain's quartz monadnock resonates
subtly in pebbles and nervous systems,
twelve miles west, a crystal set transmitter
upthrust two billion years ago, urging
vowels on evolving brains. Vibrations,
whale songs tease fillings. My teeth are a white
xylophone of voices. Exorcisms,
yoga, dentists yield before this yawning
zoo of noises—the inner sphere's Muzak.

BABBLE'S TOWER

An angelic dot-to-dot, your face's
beam of light darts tree-road-river-cloud-sky,
connects them in a glib web. "In detox,
despair taught me God might not exist. However, faith's real." I pass an SUV,
fat guy driving, wire-thin goatee, as you
go on, staticky. "Faith can levitate
Himalayan Mountains blocking our minds.
Indian rope trick we use to reach our
Jupiter selves. You can raise your I.Q."
Kindred souls on cell phones. You say, "Large cup
latte with extra cream" in Chicago.
Meanwhile I drive to work in Wisconsin,
note the plastic badger for you, his home
on top of the exotic dance club. Whole
paragraphs stacked between us, blocks of talk
quixotically tilt. "QMAJ
relay tower ahead," you announce. I
say, "Dad built ham radios. A mammoth
tower in our backyard. Weekends sitting
up late talking to England, France. Bits of
voices bouncing around the atmosphere."
"We had four-leaf clovers in our backyard!
Extra luck. But during storms, I'd panic,"
you confess. "That's where lightning'd always stab."
"Zeus was just jealous of your luck," I say.

Power Lunch

"Accept no substitutes. King of all sins.
Big kick in God's balls, egged on by envy.
Cardinal sin from which the other six
deadly sins spawn. It all starts with pride. How
else could anything exist? Pride, not love,
formed us. Our starry ball set rolling thru
God's grand commandment of 'Let there be light!'
His sin is universal. The Devil's
infinitesimal. But Lucifer?
Judged for hubris. Cast from Heaven. Unique
keeper of God's guilt, who with one misstep
lost face and gained a scapegoat's goat feet. No
more gazing on God's countenance. Begin-
ning of evil. But which of them's to blame?
On this point, theologians still waffle."
Putting blackberry jam on mine, I ask
Quist, my tutelary demon and sage,
"Really? After all, we're fighting God. I
still don't see how we can win, even though
the world's going to hell in a brown bag."
Umber smoke curls from her smile. Olive loaf,
Velveeta cheese and mayo on dark rye.
"Win?" Quist gobbles some fries, slurps a malted.
"Excellent plan. We piss on the lilacs,
yet Yahweh persists." We toast Beelzebub,
zebub of gluttony, with a loud bray.

KEY LIME CHRIST

Ziploc bag of void, vacuum-packed with Zen's
yes to the abyss. Numb embrace. Empty
ecstasies. Glass half full of near beer. Sex
without climax. The cosmic egg hollow.
Vampiric Dalai Lama child beams love—
umbilical leads to a baby, blue,
thrown out with the bath since "All life is just
suffering." Orange robes swarm the U.S.,
recruit on campuses. Islam's martyr
quotes God, then blows himself up in Iraq.
Pays lives for his afterlife brides. An imp
occupies the Pope's hat—that white silo.
No Catholic, I collect Spider-Man.
My wife sits home and tithes "our" income. Some
Latin American mission's rice bowl
kept full by Church of Christ with my paycheck.
Joann and Jesus spend a sinner's wage.
I flex free will, no patience of Job. I
hit the road, backseat full of comix. Both
God and my ex left holding the mortgage.
For now I'll bet against an afterlife.
Each and every one true god can go be
damned. I'll worship ice cream, multi-flavored.
Chanting as I drive, I'm my own cleric.
Baskin-Robbins, next exit. Mint fudge bomb.
Almond abyss. Peanut butter Buddha.

LEVITATION BREATHING

Ass spasms briefly snap yogic flyers'
bodies up. Heaven's hope a hop away.
Called levitation, though jumping beans Mex
do the same tricks. The magician's shadow
escaped. Earth-bound, it shrinks. The secret of
flight hangs like an apple in front of you.
Grab it. Only $19.95. Just
have your credit card ready. The Chinese
in '06 hung a minnow in mid-air—
jelled sea of sound waves of a certain freq.
Kept it there curled in a waterless gasp.
Lifted in magnetic fields years ago,
mice wore metal belts. That communist minnow's not the first levitation victim.
130,000 results will
pop up on an internet search. One link:
quarried blocks Merlin floated to Stonehenge,
raising them stately as zeppelins. I
say water-walking counts. My Navy hitch
taught me air hockey, the puck hovering.
You walked on water as a sailor if
evaluations glowed, perfect. I breathe,
walls of my ribcage race out, lungs swell, mind
expands, that genie's bottle, magnetic
yolk sac, its walls half an atom thin. Ab-
surd balloon holding us, drifting away.

Lost & Found

A bright child dreaming his missing mitten's
become a goldfish, swimming a linty
cube of scarves, hats, coats. The lost & found box.
Dorsal fin a thumb he snags it by. "Wow!"
Evan's 1ˢᵗ grade hand touched by the god of
Found Again. God with a little g. You
go past miracles all the time but just
haven't noticed how Hermes, god of thieves,
instigates your lost car keys. He later
jangles them in your pocket. Or not. Pique
keeps the gods' good deeds in check. So suck up.
Light some incense like the ancients did, who
made peace with sky, tree, sea and hill. They brown-
nosed every clover patch for good luck from
Odin's day on down, but it made them kneel.
Polytheism named our days of the week,
quivers the woods with souls called trees. Blue jays,
robins, swine that were human once. Omniscient for a fee, the local priest or witch
tried crystal balls, pendulums and dowsing
until recently to find your lost stuff.
Viviane kept and keeps a king's sword safe
while Arthur's body sleeps between planes, wrapped,
exempt from time, till needed. Specific
yet unnamed, this deity I would dub
Zephta, keeper of what's lost, tucked away.

BLACK PYRAMID

Zoetrope god spins, resulting in lives,
years, movements. The world as optical toy.
Exhibit A: soul as special FX.
Weightless whiteness. Brief puff behind the brow.
Vestigial, if it exists. Most of
us don't use it. Lose it. Adieu, virtue.
The possessed, exorcised of free will, float
same as saints. Not much difference these days.
Rent a movie from that new sub-genre
quickly filling shelves. "Torture porn." Grotesque
perversions and mutilations worked up-
on women. Priests molesting children. Who
knows where it'll end? Not television,
mental mosquito distracting us from
looking up and noticing that black hole
kept in check by science, magic and luck.
Juvenile diabetes soars. The urge
in charge. Binge/purge = fasting. INRI
had his day. Now we place our faith in cash.
Gluttony. Safe sex. Zombies start moving
faster in movies, then rise in real life.
Estates revert back to them. This time the
dead are the ones building the pyramid,
church leaders strangely mute on the topic.
Bored, we hit the buffet at Adam's Rib
as corpses push stone blocks up ramps all day.

OVER THE RAINBOW

Aeons of apes get stomach aches because
black-and-white sight can't see ripeness. The sky
changes gradually. Primate eyes coax
dull gray into light blue. First to see how
Eden's apples blushed like flesh, ape-girl Eve
fed all of us from God's green grove. Can you
guess who saw the first pale rainbow? A rust-
honey monkey named Dorothy. Ancients,
in their mosaics, lacked purple. They were
just unable to see it. An opaque
kaleidoscope with gaps, our vision's map
lags behind birds, bees, fish, rats. Half the zoo
moves through an ultraviolet realm un-
known except by UV lens or a storm
on the way: lime clouds, blood grass, gray hail. Hell
posing for its pink-lit portrait. A crack
quivers in the window. A dazed blue jay
reverts to gray. Colors bleed from my eyes,
stick to my cheeks like rainbow syrup. Bosch
triptych landscape minus sinners. A gong
undulates. Stars shift across a red gulf.
Evolution revokes rainbows from some
white males, 8% of them color blind.
Xanthic, now, the Golden Age. Myopic,
yawning, I water the lawn, the rhubarb.
Oz fades. My hose's rainbow dims, goes gray.

LANDSCAPE WITH SINNERS

Zooplastic figures. A wasp's head drones buzz-
y speech from a naked woman's body.
X-rated marriage of parts. Pig sports tux.
Weird Tree of Life, sculpted, pink as a sow.
Viewed from safe distance. Year 1505.
Unearthly garden of delights seen thru
the brush of Hieronymus Bosch. His art
still brightens break room walls in Tartarus.
Rockwellian, for hell. Norman's down there,
quietly working, as well. Same technique,
picturesque grown pithy. An orange imp
oversees his latest: tarnished halo
notched, an alter boy kneels and prays. White gown,
maroon spot on his bum. Priest leers, straight from
Lovecraft's story "Pickman's Model." A ghoul
kingdom under the graveyards of New York.
Jaundiced fiends, at feast, rendered by one J.
Inman Pickman, who paints from photos. I
hear about the cloaked, hooded figures Bosch
glimpsed. They left huge rooster tracks. Demons hang
fresh sinners by thumbs, tongues, genitals. Stuff
embers in holes. Each generation re-
designs Hell. Touring saints ignore the damned.
Catholic renaissance triptych comic
books. *Mad*'s back cover fold-ins. Human limb
attached to lobster. Claws attempt to pray.

Raising Hell

"…as there's no way to safely summon A-
baddon, whose guidance is needed to plumb
certain depths of the abyss. Since magic
demands sacrifice, once summoned, the fiend
eviscerates with malefic glee the
first magician, tearing him/her in half,
gorging on guts, distracted. Not for long,
however. With alacrity, 'Yod Heh
In Heh' is intoned by the *Put that Oui-
ja board away, Mr. Pierce!* second mage,
keeping it at bay while others (the Black
Lodge recommends four operators, all
Major Adepts) trace sigils and wards, form
numinous bands, the key of Solomon
of course binding it, allowing us to
pose our queries for one hour. Once time's up,
questions end. Abaddon fades. His oblique
replies requiring analysis for
syllogistical inconsistencies.
These martyrs help map the bottomless pit,
uncharted well of Heaven's umbrage. U.
V. light pours from its mouth, a desert cave
witching the stars with violet, pink. Few
except us know where it is. Lux onyx.
Yogis seek the light trapped in dark: aby-
ssal Lucifer, his astral Alcatraz."

Black Lodge

"… and, since we've managed to suspend karma,
birth and rebirth, time and death, our will's web
circles the globe. At its hub, sulfuric
demiurge Beelzebub, tentacled
emptiness, Satan's second, whom entire
family lines have served since the dawn of
Gnosticism. Before man came along,
Hell had a deal with dinosaurs. Such flesh!
If you've tasted it you won't touch sushi.
Juxtaposed with us since then, the White Lodge,
kind of a karmic police force. Our black
lodgers battling Himalayan astral
masters. Let's just say they don't have the same
notion of order we do. They come on
our campus every fall semester to
proselytize. We let them set up shop,
quote scripture, while their campus in Dubuque
returns the favor, our own recruiter
seducing whom she may, ripe succubus.
They all drink her bathwater in secret
under their chapel. Meanwhile, you plod thru
volumes. Visualize. Deny the grave.
Work frees you to live fully on Earth. How
exquisite, this ball of shit—clay phoenix
Yahweh wastes on man. Next week, we study
Zagan, Hell's Duke, whose bull head turns fools wise."

Winter Radio

After work I putz around the house. "Maybe Hell's real," says Brent from Detroit. "Maybe
Choronzon rules the abyss. Catholic
doctrine tells us the devil exists, and
exorcists…" A blast of static. "…where she
floated just below the ceiling in Af-
ghanistan for thirteen hours straight and sang
'Happy Days Are Here Again' in Spanish."
It's January in WI.
"Just keep your dial tuned to WJ
KU, AM 690." Busy work.
Little projects so I don't go nuts. I'll
maybe paint the bathroom window frame. Tom,
north Texas cabbie, calls on his cell phone:
"Only pure silver, molten, poured into
pentagrams carved in a stone floor can trap
Qliphoth-spawned demons. This is the technique
ritually used by the Black Lodge for
summonings." By five-thirty the window's
tar black. Standing in the bathtub, I paint
until I've squared the formless darkness, view
void framed by pale yellow, the color of
wisdom. "…like batteries. Once angels, now
exhibits. Lead to gold. Incubus sex.
Yoked forces." Buzzed on fumes in my holy
zone, I see demons, trapped like damaged Gods.

SIGNATURE PIECE

Zephyrs left her lips as she sang time's sea.
Yin-yang, once begun, made chaos succumb.
Expelled stardust from her subatomic
womb spun stars. Angels came later. Finished
vibrating her name's web, she slept/sleeps. The
unified theory we seek is belief,
tying everything together: faith's string
Satan tugs. Say God's name backwards and cloth
raveled unravels again through magi
quantum mystery mechanics. Black Lodge
paladins aid Lucifer's cause: to seek
out pieces of God's name, work to re-spool
nimbus clouds like used wool from old quilts, com-
mand wheat fields to unstitch, snowflakes to un-
lace from each other, float heavenward. To
know where to look takes talent. There's an imp
jokingly called "Truffles." Super I.Q.,
if somewhat porcine. But in the last four
hundred years Hell's swine sniffed out three letters.
Geese. Sunlight's script on water. Fire. The first
few are easy. Cavemen knew them. But you
earn the rest. So far the devil has twelve.
Despondent, the Crow of Doom waits to caw
chaos, antimatter's anticlimax,
big bang blown backwards. What's behind the sky?
Atoms big as bees. Existential buzz.

JANUS CAVE

Auschwitz ashes and the Mona Lisa,
both from the same bipolar God, whose glib
clerics get Him off the hook. Fine gray talc
drifts down from above. Not His fault. All good
emanates from Heaven. We're evil. Blame
free will. Pass the buck. Invent Satan. "If
God's real, the buck stops with the one in charge!"
Hank's my stepdad. Retired Army. His faith
is tempered by time in Korea. "I
judge right back!" Later, while mopping O.J.
Kevin spilled, I'm glad to have stress-free work:
little kids, teachers, corndogs. All's dual.
My deity's Janus of ancient Rome,
noted for his two faces, transition,
one condition to another. Also
portals, doors—which janitors unlock, wipe.
"Quonset huts in January. No liq-
uor. Frozen mud," Hank says. I come over
sometimes and we have a few beers. He talks,
ticks off dead friends, pinkie lost to frostbite
useful again. Recalls an impromptu
vacation: an hour's pause in a mud cave
where an arm stabbed the wall, hand to elbow
exposed, frozen pole. "You smoke…joke…relax.
You don't feel anything. That's what's scary.
Zahn hung a lamp from that arm. Like the Ritz."

Janus Calf

Anton Schmidtbauer as a boy held a
blind two-headed calf and felt its life ebb.
Couldn't see why it was born. God's logic
didn't make much sense to him that day and
eventually made even less. He
fought in World War Two. Thought about that calf.
Got bronze and silver stars for valor. Dug
holes to sleep in, fighting Rommel. 7th
Infantry. Africa. Italy. "I
judged Heaven, in that foxhole. God won't change.
Killing's His job." He's eighty now. We talk
like this sometimes. Drink. "Maybe the evil
men do pleases Heaven. The good, too." From
now on, each afternoon when I come in
on my janitor's shift, I make sure to
pat Jimmy's hand in a high-five. I slap.
Quack. He quacks back from his wheelchair, I.Q.
range normal, just another 1st grader,
skewed by cerebral palsy. The Powers
That Be may have screwed this cheerful kid, but
you and I (free will) can still show virtue—
vacant Heaven better than God of love
who sacrifices to Himself. A few
ex-Jews small price to feed this sunset's sex-
y oven. Hitler painted roses. Why?
Zebra God alike of Eden, Auschwitz.

Ragnarok

At the edge of creation sits an a-
bandoned construction site: slabs of prefab
clouds; rusted stacks of unlit zodiac;
dump trucks piled with cosmic dust; some dented,
empty paint cans labeled "Eden Green"; crane
for arranging planets. Before belief,
gods worked here, building worlds without end. Hung
Heaven's dreaming ceiling. Then quit. That hush
is what's left—shadows licking things. Loki
jeers, spits wine at a dying fire, barks "J!
Kindling!" Cement bags blow across the dark
lot. Christ comes back in work boots, with a pail.
Monkey bones burn just as well as wood. "From
now on, use the wheelbarrow!" the raven
on Odin's shoulder croaks. Odin tries to
point, but he's drunk, falls in the fire. Goes up
quick as sawdust. "I just blessed a new mosque!"
rejoices Allah, stepping from thin air.
"Say, what *is* that smell?" The almost endless
twilight of the gods is almost done, but
until the Crow of Doom caws, no adieu.
Venus, gazing at Earth, feels a trace of
wonder at our blue wish of a world. "Caw!"
exults the crow, brandishing a Rolex
winding down on its wrist. Cursing, crusty
Zeus follows Odin and sparks the last blaze.

POPULATION CLOCK

Xerox copier that's stuck on print as
you watch life swell in '08, by July
exceeding 6.66 billion. Sex
will finish us—unless they're all somehow
virgin births sent by God to plague us, starve
us, drought us. Forget the avian flu,
the threat of meteors like the one that
smote the dinosaurs back when we were rats
running rings around their rooster feet, or
quakes or flames or floods or wars in Iraq,
Pakistan, Iran. I tell myself, stop
obsessing on omega. Did Nero?
No. He just played on, like those nine or ten
musicians manning the Titanic, calmly crazy. Canceling the future will
kill unborn billions. We dropped to 10K
just this last glacial age, taking refuge
in ice caves, on extinction's edge, yeti
hunting us like some animal. The South
gets warm. Gray spores smothering an orange,
fruitfully we multiply, holding life,
each life, precious while killing for a mate,
dominion, dollars. Our own nest so fouled
cancer's running rampant, etc.
Balance survival with compassion. Ab-
andon responsibility and pray.

Viral Savior

All those SUVs racing A to Z
burn dead dinosaurs, fueled by war. Why
care? The end is near, here. A plague, a pox.
Ducks in a row. Slot machine windows show
every time the darkly dotted line of
flu-bearing birds bisecting blue sky. Flu
germs drop like bombs from feathered bellies, halt
history, abort tomorrow. Soon nukes
in Nebraska will rust, mutate future
jackalope and deer herds. We're not unique—
killed off if Earth wobbles wrong. Time to stop
lying to ourselves, our place in things no
more secure than hummingbirds' flicker, in-
nocent of hypertension. Meanwhile I'm
optimistic a UFO fleet will
plunge up from the sea. The saucers will look
quite a bit like carnival glass. They'll judge
our best worthy of relocation. I
saw all this in a vision. Huge ships, each
the size of Gilligan's Island, flying
under the direction of our lord of
viruses Jesus Christ, and in time we
will make sitcoms about how we escaped,
except some won't laugh, will call it tragic,
why most died. Of our own genocide absolved. A virus saved us on Judgment Day.

Night School

Zeno lectures in my sleep. "The sun as
you know is a great bowl filled with fiery
exhalations." I learn warm mud sexes
worms and flies and frogs from nothingness, how
vapors condense, form water, then earth. Wave
undulates into stone. Quartz seas wash thru
the earth. Time's granite tide rocks at our feet.
Some of us have a few drinks after class,
rant, rage, bullshit, explicate. Before our
quorum breaks up, we toast ourselves—truth's clique.
Pure reason dipped in wit. Two patrons clap.
"Our riches have destroyed us. Old Plato
never had this problem. We're a nation
mostly of children," bitches that old ham
Lucretius. "The people all have dimple
knees in my country," I echo. "Few work,
just hover above buffets and suck fudge.
In some cases their faces explode." I
hitch my toga. Seneca gives a belch.
"Gods!" He staggers. "What else?" Another tug.
Friggin' toga's crooked. "The marriage of
evolution and natural science
delivers wonders," I declaim, "undreamed.
Capturing brief puffs of the sun's epic
breath, each spark is sealed in a small glass orb,
and banishing darkness, night becomes day!"

Tree of Life

Air scarred, like quartz, like a lightning bolt froze.
Asleep, oblivious as Lazarus
and the commotion unheard (if there was
any) announcing the birdbath's demise.
An emanationist example: cause
and effect. God's pinkie finger descends
almightily, right where my garage was,
as Heaven's nail pierces sky, pins lawn, binds
all to each. I reach out before my brain's
aware what's happening. My palm just slides
away. Some kind of force field. The neighbors
aren't up yet. It's Sunday. Instead of leaves,
a dozen globes, maybe big as TVs,
aquariums where rainbows swim like eels
alive and ribboning. The highest orbs
are pure light, but as they descend their blaze
abates. Light gets dressed in dirt. Kabbalah's
arbor vitae risen overnight, beans
are what spring to mind. Magic beans. Ego's
apart, a screen to come between what is
and what I see no longer. Useless as
an appendix. Devoid of lies, vision's
awful, won at the cost of the eye, selves
and memories exhausted, shed, my heart's
abyss unwrapped of oniony layers,
approaching sirens—the buzz of what *is*.

HITLER ROSES

Abstinence evolves another species
below the radar, as celibacy
causes some to wed their own souls, their sex
drives defused, used instead to paint, write—however that green genie of creative
force chooses to manifest, breaking thru
greedy layers of ego. Those who fast
happily slip past curved white bars of bones,
invisibly free of McHamburger
jowls, fat's quilt of gravity. In Iraq,
Kristallnacht: this time, roadside bombs. Misstep—
leaving the hot light behind, each one's "no"
martyred on the air, fog in desert sun.
"No," I echo. I unbecome a womb
of vacuum, letting go. Less. Less, until
profligate nature abhors me, my blank
quietism. An agnostic gnostic, Maj-
or Mike of an ascetic army, I
swell with absences and rise like hot ash,
trailing a comic book cape of flowing
undersea murk to alleviate grief,
vice and virtue. Dark as a shark's dead eye,
waves eclipse the sun's goatish iris, gold
extinguished. I levitate, amnesic,
yet remembering roses' red scent, absolved of self, odor rising through smoke's sea.

Cattle Mutilations

A Navy buddy finds me: we trade calls
biweekly. "A Midwest delicacy,
cow tongue is Heaven's Spam," I brag. Steve Cox
died once—allergic shock from a cashew.
EMTs saved him. "I was wrapped in love
for six months. Dressed in bliss…unable to
give a shit, knowing that all things work out,"
he says, from Seattle. "Drove Annette nuts."
I laugh. Mr. Peanut as Zen master.
"Jellied cow's blood sausage," I say, "with cu-
cumber slices, salt and mustard on top."
"Little gray men fly all the way here to
make a sandwich," Steve quips. "Been going on
now since '61. Eyes, tongue, lungs, rectum.
One minute's work with a laser scalpel,
piece of rye and they're gone. The starry black
quilt above Kansas your witness; their fridge
restocked." We laugh, and Steve starts to cough. I
say nothing. He was a nuke missile tech,
Trident subs. Each lung's a wet paper bag:
unshielded radiation. "Forget grief.
Every day is a gift." Then he tells me,
"World War One, Grandpa and Hitler both gassed,
exact same battle. Gramps lived, asthmatic.
Yperite: mustard gas." Mist becomes web.
Zyklon B…cattle cars…"Breathe in each day."

ADAM AGAIN

As I shave, my face bursts into flames—bronze
blaze bright as the sun in the mercury
cube of the mirror. I laugh, half-shaved, ex-
drunken sailor, my old Dixie cup now
exclamation points of light, a crown of
flame, Heaven's wedding ring. Tomorrow you
get to wear it. And the day after that?
Who knows? A halo that's passed around. Saints
incognito, queens in disguise linger
just behind you, getting cones at DQ.
King for a day, now it's my turn to clap,
laugh, point and name things: creation's ego-
maniac. Adam all over again,
naming an Indian elephant "Om-
ophant" this time around. God's holy fool.
Poster boy for creation, karma blank.
Qabbalah's Adam Kadmon, my lips conj-
uring names fast as hummingbird farts. I
say "Minnesota"—swallows wheel on high
toward their new destination. I sing
"Ursa Major"—a favor to bears. Laugh
violently. Then I begin to name
whole galaxies for gay couples. "Bob/Fred
Xl9," I pronounce, squinting. "Eric/
Yasha 3." Stars begin swarming like bees.
Zebras sport unicorn horns for a day.

SUNLIGHT MONSTER

Aleister (The Beast) Crowley: "Death's in a-
beyance while we live, and from Adam's ribcage sprang breasts. (Did you know he was A/C
D/C? Swang both ways. Hermaphrodite!) Old
Epicurus was right. You, me—we live
forever in our minds. A minute's life
gone the next. No ego overlapping
here and now and the hereafter. When death
is present, we're absent. So you and I
just became immortal. If I misjudge,
kill me. God will. Starting right now, this week,
let's live like we'll live forever, like al-
mighty gods. Our technology brings om-
nipresence closer daily, each cell phone
one more voice in universal echo.
Poems sprout on shopping bags. You look up
quick enough to see the sun's Rubenesque
reflection of mankind's face. Our souls are
swamp gas, ball lightning, freakish consciousness
that hovers a short while above the dust.
Use us. Under love nothing is tabu.
Voodoo of the white man, whose juju love
works his will on the world. Love is the law
exalted. Climaxed, our Golden Dawn's sex-
y firebomb lights the abyss. Finally
zombies enlightened. A new race of gods."

THE POSSESSED

aren't like that. No pre-teen girls floating a-
bove their beds, wearing pea-soup puke, green dab
clinging to one cheek. Way too dramatic.
Demons don't work that way. That's Hollywood.
Evil doesn't go where it's not welcome.
Forget the Polish parish priest's belief
God dwells in a cookie. The possessed chug
holy water, piss vinegar—prove faith
is where you find it. Or not. FYI:
Jesus? Possessed by light. Others use maj-
ick to gain self-possession, not unlike
Lord Vader's offer to young Luke to rule
millions of worlds, bring order between them—
another metaphor for discipline
of self. Perfect possession takes years to
perfect. Fear, love and desire offered up.
Quartzite from the heart's seat hums. The I.Q.
rises, as does the subconscious. The more
sacrificed, the more gained. Odin gave his
torn-out eye to a demon for insight,
understanding. Apprenticed to the universe, we evolve, serve the creative
will; burn at the heart of the world for now—
exiled for refusing the crucifix.
Yet all's well. We serve Hell's will, ours paraly-
zed by joy's low-voltage seven-hertz buzz.

GILGAMESH TOMB FOUND IN IRAQ

"O, it turns out the sonofabitch and
narcissist is immortal after all…"
                    —Karl Elder in "Gilgamesh at the Bellagio"

Abuzz with conspiracy theories, a
blurb of truth escapes the internet's web:
cloned in secret, Gilgamesh's epic
drama resumes. He returns from the dead.
Expedition led by Germans finds the
fabled city, Uruk. The Persian Gulf
gets invaded one month later, nothing
heard again. Same way the UFO crash
in Roswell spawned one headline. FYI
Jesus is coming—He's one pissed-off judge.
Know, O Prince, King Gilgamesh shall come back
like Arthur, but this returning royal
murders mankind's future with Nephilim,
New World Order orchestrating return
of this demigod to the throne, also
priest, star of oldest known poem, Hell's imp,
Qliphoth's knight. Doom's clap sounding from Iraq
resonates thy greatness, Son of Sumer,
son who saw the abyss, crossed the abyss
to defeat death. The U.S. Government
unearthed your remains, found (no Enkidu)
viable alien DNA. Grave
warriors seed Armageddon's shadow.
X-Files becomes real. We fight a phoenix.
Yea, though I be the only one to pray,
Zeus save us from extinction's losing buzz.

Author's Bio

Winner of *North American Review's* Hearst Poetry Prize and numerous other awards, Michael Kriesel is the poetry editor of *Rosebud* magazine. His work appears in the 2017 anthology *New Poetry from the Midwest* (New American Press). A past President of the Wisconsin Fellowship of Poets, his poems and reviews have appeared in *Alaska Quarterly Review, Antioch Review, Library Journal, Rattle, The Progressive, Small Press Review,* and *Wisconsin People & Ideas.* Read his electronic chapbook of short poems, *Every Name in the Book,* at www.righthandpointing.net/michael-kriesel-every-name.

34509234R00057

Made in the USA
Middletown, DE
28 January 2019